AF481098

This book belongs to

....

Journey for a Better Life

The story of Jose and Angelina

Written by

Richard José Pérez

Illustrations by Blueberry Illustrations

DEDICATION

To My Loving Family,

My heartfelt gratitude goes to my wife, Maria, and our daughter, Amanda, whose support, editing, and feedback made this book shine. Your patience and insights to this project transformed it into something beautiful.

To my dearest sister, Sylvia, you provided the missing pieces to this story, the intricate details that brought it to life. Your wisdom and memories have enriched this book in ways words cannot express.

This book is a testament to the love and strength of our family, including all José and Angelina's descendants. You are the heart and soul of this story.

Keep working toward a brighter future for generations to come and making valuable contributions to our nation.

In 1952, José and Angelina met in Morelia, a beautiful city in Mexico. Angelina was 19 and spent her days working at a tortilla factory, while 29-year-old José earned his living by selling charcoal he personally made from forest trees. Their lives were full of hard work, low wages, and the weight of poverty. Yet, in the midst of these challenges, José dreamed of a better life, not only for himself but also for the family he envisioned having with Angelina someday.

Tortillería Morelia
TAXI

One sunny day, José visited the *tortillería* where Angelina worked. With a hopeful smile, he shared his dream of going to America and asked Angelina to come along. "Let's go to the United States," José excitedly told Angelina. "It's a beautiful place, and there are lots of jobs waiting for us." Angelina wasn't quite ready to say yes, but deep down, she understood that going to America could lead them out of poverty. Even though it meant venturing into the unknown and leaving their loved ones behind, they set out on a journey to find a better life.

José got permission to enter the United States, but he was not able to obtain one for Angelina. They faced a difficult decision: either remain in Mexico, struggling with not having enough food and money, or attempt to enter the United States. They realized that once their journey began, there would be no turning back.

Then suddenly one night, José said to Angelina, "*Vamonos*, let's go. We need to try to cross to the other side." So José and Angelina set out on their new journey. They took a big risk and decided to cross the Rio Grande River, driven by the hope of finding a better life. This was an exceptionally brave action, even though they were aware it would be dangerous.

Crossing the river at the border was really risky. Angelina had to fight hard to stay safe because the powerful river currents tried to sweep her away. "Hold onto the tree branch," José shouted, guiding Angelina through the wild river. Amazingly, they reached the other side. Years later, José would share this story with their children, and Angelina would shake her head, covering her ears, as her husband told the frightening story again.

The couple settled in Texas, where José's strong work ethics earned him the trust of his boss, who in turn helped secure permanent legal status for both José and Angelina in the United States. By this time, they had a family of five children. José worked irrigating the cotton fields and picking cotton, while Angelina managed household tasks, caring for their children, and preparing meals. In the evenings, they made tacos, and José would venture out to sell them on the streets late into the night, providing the much-needed extra income. "May God help you sell those tacos," Angelina would tell José.

16

In the 1950s, Texas had some rules that weren't fair to Mexicans. José remembers he got paid less just because he was Mexican. He also saw signs on buildings that said "No Mexicans Allowed." One day, he heard about a place called California that might be better. "Let's go to California! People say there are lots of jobs there," José told Angelina. Angelina wasn't sure at first, but she would do anything for a chance of a better life for her children.

Under the scorching July sun, with the hot wind blowing harshly, the couple and their five children found themselves riding in the back of a pickup truck for days. The journey to California stretched out long and ended up being a dreadful experience for the couple. Angelina was concerned for their safety. "I'm worried about the children," Angelina confided to José, her voice burdened with anxiety. "The winding roads and the cliffs are frightening." Suddenly, her worst fear came true, and she cried out, "*Dios mío* (Oh, my God)!" as another vehicle crashed into their truck. The truck almost tipped over the edge of the cliff, making everything extremely frightening. But they were all safe.

After traveling for nearly a week in the back of the pickup truck, they finally arrived one day at dusk and spent their first night in California under a fig tree next to a tall, white monument in the Central Valley. José would later tell his kids that his first home in California was a treehouse. After several days under the fig tree, they were offered housing at a farm labor camp in Merced County.

For years, José and Angelina lived in the Central Valley with their seven daughters and six sons. They had bittersweet days in California. José's sweet days came from taking his children to the fields to teach them to work hard and earn a living. For Angelina, it involved preparing meals for her children and making sure they all made it to school. They had their share of sadness and disappointments, like seeing one of their sons become very ill in his younger years and then losing him to cancer as an adult.

Still, José and Angelina had a lot to be thankful for and were proud of their children. They always knew their decision to come to America was the right one. "You need to be grateful for your father's vision to come to America," Angelina would tell her children. And they never forgot it.

José and Angelina's descendants now number over 140 and counting, all of them with their hearts full of love and gratitude for the courage and sacrifice of José and Angelina. They all hope for a better life for their children, just as José and Angelina did. Whether they become teachers, nurses, scientists, or entrepreneurs, the descendants of this remarkable couple will continue to inspire future generations in this land of opportunity, where José and Angelina's dream of a better tomorrow lives on.

About the Author

Richard José Pérez, a lifelong educator, has been captivated by his parents' journey to the United States for many years. As his father shared details of their remarkable journey, Richard's fascination deepened. Eager to honor his parents' sacrifices for a better future, Richard wanted all the family's descendants to know the story of José and Angelina. Through his writing, Richard recognized the universal resonance of his narrative, echoing the experiences of countless immigrants seeking a better life in America.